CONTENTS

The History of
The Friars
Aylesford

Front Cover: The Friars; *engraving dated 1792*

INTRODUCTION

In many ways, the story of The Friars is the story of God writing straight with crooked lines. It is a story of hope, of new beginnings and also, at times, of seeming disaster.

The first Carmelites who came to Aylesford in the thirteenth century were given a frosty welcome, but they persevered and their Priory was soon a house of prayer which was valued by the surrounding population.

Religious change under Henry VIII drove the Carmelites out of Aylesford, and The Friars was set to follow countless other abbeys and priories across the land in becoming a picturesque ruin. Fortunately, the monastic buildings found a domestic use and The Friars became the home of various Kentish families, though not without a brush with turbulent events.

At the beginning of this century Mrs Woolsey's loving care saved the buildings from decay. However, fire and the Second World War almost undermined that care. Then, some 50 years ago, the Carmelites realised a dream when they were able to purchase their old home. In 1949, Father Malachy Lynch and his fellow friars began the work of restoring The Friars.

Restoration continues today, and The Friars has become, through popular support, a great centre of pilgrimage and a place of ecumenical activity. It is one of the few medieval religious houses that is once again in the hands of its founding order – the Carmelites or Whitefriars. We hope you enjoy reading this history of The Friars and its many inhabitants.

THE FOUNDING YEARS

The Carmelite Order has its origins in groups of hermits living on Mount Carmel who were given a Rule between 1208 and 1214 by Albert, the Patriarch of Jerusalem. The hermits, inspired by the Prophet Elijah, had congregated on Mount Carmel and from there began to go out and preach in the coastal towns of the Holy Land. However, the territory won for Christianity by the Crusaders was gradually taken over by the Saracens, and some of the hermits were only too pleased to accept the English Crusaders' offer to bring them to England.

The story of The Friars at Aylesford began in 1242, when Richard de Grey gave a group of Carmelite hermits from the Holy Land a small piece of marshy land at his manor of Aylesford, near the River Medway just north-west of the village and three miles from Maidstone. The newcomers were not welcomed with open arms by the local population, and it was 1247 before Richard of Wendover, the Bishop of Rochester, recognised the new Order.

The first few years must have been difficult. It seems that the Carmelites built a small chapel and some individual cells, possibly of wood, near the river where the present Choir Chapel is situated. For the first few years they had no official status – at best they were guests of the de Grey family. The Church had put an embargo on founding new orders in 1215 as there had been a rash of new groups. The Carmelites had received their Rule before then, but it was not easy for a small group of poor men to press their case. In the end, the Bishop of Rochester accepted the validity of their position and in 1247 gave them permission to build a church and establish a religious house. More importantly, he encouraged benefactors by awarding 30 days' indulgence to those who contributed to the work.This recognition came in January 1247, which was to be a deeply significant year for the Carmelites, as the first General Chapter of the Order outside the Holy Land took place at Aylesford. The Chapter elected a Brother Godfrey as the Prior General, but more importantly it began a process that would transform the Carmelites from hermits to mendicant friars. The hermit way of life was full of difficulties, above all in finding suitable places to live and benefactors to support communities. The Carmelites were now being offered sites in the towns of Western Europe with patrons ready to help them. Two Carmelites, Peter and Reginald, were sent to Pope Innocent IV with a request to change The Rule of St Albert. Two Dominican friars, Cardinal Hugh of St Caro and a Bishop William, considered the request and on their advice the Pope allowed modifications to be made to The Rule. The Carmelites were allowed to make foundations in towns and a greater emphasis was placed on community life. In effect, the Carmelites joined the ranks of the mendicant friars who were moving into towns and universities. This was not popular with everyone and produced tensions between those who saw a life of prayer and solitude as faithful to the Order's vision and those who saw prayer and service as parts of a seamless whole.

It is in this context that St Simon Stock appears. Very few hard facts are known about him, but he is an important figure in the story of the Order. He appears to have been one of the early Priors General of the Order and died in Bordeaux. His surname

Below: The Arrival of the Carmelites *by Adam Kossowski*

indicated that he could have come from Kent – either Stoke in the Isle of Grain or Stockbury near Sittingbourne. He is seen as a supporter of the change in the Carmelites' way of life from being hermits to becoming friars. The story has it that while he was at prayer, Mary, the Mother of God, appeared to him in a vision and promised her protection to the new Order, saying that the scapular, part of the Carmelite habit, would be the sign of her protection. Simon's vision is held to have taken place at Aylesford in 1251. This episode cannot be proved historically, but the tradition is important in the Carmelite story nonetheless and has inspired great devotion to Mary, the Mother of God, both within the Order and in the Church at large.

The Carmelites were also beneficiaries of royal generosity in 1247, when Henry III gave two marks towards the cost of the General Chapter that had recently been held at Aylesford. Richard de Grey also helped the Carmelites' finances at this time by making an agreement between the Carmelites and the

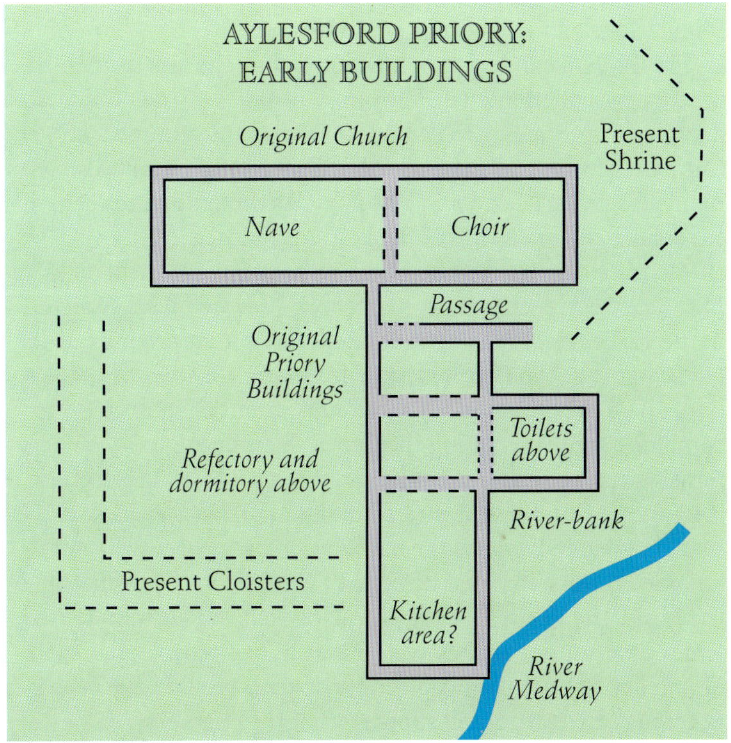

Rectors of Aylesford parish church. The living at Aylesford was held by the Master of the hospital at Strood and he was anxious that tithes for burials and services should not be lost. Richard de Grey pledged that he would pay in perpetuity a sum of 12 shillings to offset any loss of offerings.

On 31 August 1248, Richard of Wendover, the Bishop of Rochester, dedicated the first Church at the Priory in honour of the Blessed Virgin Mary of Mount Carmel and in honour of the Assumption of the Glorious Virgin. The dedication was one of the first in England under the title of The Assumption of Mary, and reflected a devotion that the Carmelites had brought from the Holy Land. The dedication of this small church, quite close to the river, meant that the Carmelites were officially accepted by the local Church. Over the next 50 years the Carmelite Order spread throughout the British Isles, with nearly 40 priories being established in England alone. By the end of the century Carmelites, or Whitefriars as they became known from their white cloaks, had reached as far north as Aberdeen and foundations had also been made in Ireland.

The Order's expansion in England during the late thirteenth century was phenomenal. The priory near Fleet Street in London assumed importance as a centre for studies and administration. Carmelites were well established in Oxford and Cambridge, with many becoming Masters of Theology. As the Carmelites began to settle in major centres of population they needed sound theological formation if they were to be popular preachers. Nicholas the Frenchman, in his treatise *The Fiery Arrow*, written in the 1270s, voiced his fears of uneducated friars setting out to give what they did not possess. The General Chapter of the Order held in London in 1281 and subsequent chapters tried to combine a sense of valuing the Order's hermit origins with positive steps to ensure that the brethren could be an effective force in the Church. It is interesting to note that for the first century or so in England the majority of Carmelites were not ordained priests. Besides the priories involved in the formation of the Friars, the Whitefriars in York, Norwich and Lincoln housed large communities as they were at the hub of prosperous centres of population, and the people in those cities would have been generous benefactors and supporters of the Friars.

THE MEDIEVAL CARMELITE

What was the daily routine of the medieval Carmelite friar? The first source of information would be The Rule of the Order, followed by the statutes or constitutions, and then the various decrees concerning studies. We know that for much of the medieval period there would have been about 20 friars at Aylesford. In some ways it was not a typical priory as it was in a relatively secluded situation. This meant that the spirit of solitude was more readily attained, but this element of The Rule was seen as important even in priories like London and Oxford.

The celebration of Mass was a key event in the day and would have taken place in the morning after the offices of Prime and Terce. After a collation, or breakfast, the friars would have worked until the noon office with the main meal of the day at about 3pm. Friars from a community like Aylesford would have travelled around the area preaching and supplementing the work of the local clergy.

It was usual to have some form of school attached to the priory where the basics of grammar and logic were taught. Often a priory had a friar appointed to be the lecturer. These schools were the forerunners of grammar schools and were open to all who had the leisure time to attend them, and the young friars within the Order would also have been in need of instruction. Young men joined the priory school when they were about 14 or 15, and after a period in their home priory would go on to study in either London or Oxford. The Oxford Priory was a well-organised study centre with up to 60 friars on average studying there and at the University.

Being on the Pilgrims' Way, Aylesford offered hospitality to pilgrims, so the care of visitors was important. This would have entailed the need for some sort of market garden. Monasteries and priories would usually have a herb garden as well, in order to provide medicines for the local people.

Time would have been built into the day for personal prayer and study of the scriptures, as prayerful reading of the Bible is at

De la cause de leuure emprinse.
Premier chapitre.
Pour ce que la multi
tude des liures et la
briefuete du temps et
la foiblesse du memore
ne seuffrent pas les
choses qui sont escriptes estre com
prinses ensemble en vng courage
ce mest aduis a moy qui suis le
moindre de tous mes freres en sacce.
Et ce puis ie scauoir en moymesmes
qui ay veu leu et retourne plusieurs
liures p moult long temps assiduele
ment et curieusement. Et neantmoins
par le conseil daulcuns de mes pl' sou
uerains et greigneurs aulcunes fle
que iay esleues p mon petit engin
bien pou de tous les liures de nre
foy catholique ou des liures payens.

the heart of The Rule. Many friars acted as guides and spiritual directors to the local community and were very much in demand as confessors. The friars cared for the poor but also for the great and the good!

After the office of Compline at about 7pm, the friars were bound to silence until after the morning office. This ensured peace and helped to promote a spirit of prayer.

However some of the friars would have spent time away from their priories as they went on preaching missions or carried out assignments for the Church. Because the friars took education seriously and were theologically well grounded, the Church would ask them to be bishops. Many Carmelites were suffragan bishops, carrying out the pastoral work that diocesan bishops could not do as they were so often embroiled in affairs of state.

Would the fourteenth-century friar recognise life at Aylesford today? The answer would be 'yes'. The biggest change is that we now have no office in the middle of the night, but the celebration of the Mass, the rhythm of prayer and care of people have remained constant. Then as now, the organisation of the community was democratic. The Prior, unlike an Abbot, was not

Opposite: *A medieval Carmelite in his study...*

Below: *...and his twentieth-century counterpart*

a prelate but a servant of the community, and the Chapter or Community Meeting was the forum to sort out problems and make decisions. The aim of a community of friars is to be prayerful, fraternal and open.

Carmelites down the ages have always valued silence and solitude, but not in an isolationist sense. The time for personal prayer and meditating on the Scriptures was meant to enable the individual Carmelite to bring richness and vision to his dealings with others. The ideal has always been that Carmelites should be praying communities in the midst of the people, sensitive to other peoples' needs.

Aylesford did not, however, become a backwater; over the years a number of provincial chapters were held at the priory. The de Grey family continued to be generous benefactors right up to the death of the last baron, Henry de Grey, in 1496. It would seem that for most of the medieval period there was a strong community at Aylesford, and due to local generosity the priory became a substantial building.

The Pilgrims' Hall was built around 1280 as a guest-house for pilgrims making their way to Canterbury. It was about this time that a bridge was also constructed over the Medway at Aylesford. This replaced fords and made a much more convenient crossing-point for pilgrims. The Pilgrims' Hall would have stood a little way to the south-west from the conventual buildings. It is heartening to think that this building is still a place of hospitality 700 years on.

Henry de Grey, the first Baron Codnor, proved a generous successor to Richard de Grey the founder. Between 1271 and his death in 1308 he gave land and money to the Carmelites and was summoned to Parliament in 1299, an official recognition of his status. He left a substantial sum of money to the Carmelites and this enabled them to improve the accommodation available to the community.

The records of the Rochester diocese show a constant stream of friars being ordained in the first half of the fourteenth century. Some, like Walter Browning and Roger Flete, were ordained in the Cathedral, while others were ordained in the surrounding villages: Edmund and Adam Elm were ordained at Halling, while John Berkhamstead received minor orders at Wouldham. In 1333 four friars – a deacon and three acolytes – received orders at Strood. The Rochester records indicate a close link between the friars and the villages of North Kent – a sign of the pastoral activity that must have been a hallmark of the community.

Besides the normal licensing of friars to preach and hear confessions, the Prior of Aylesford, William Hokiton, was

Right: The Building of the Church *by Adam Kossowski*

appointed by John Folsham the Provincial, in virtue of letters granted by Peter Raymond the Prior General, to preach a crusade against the Turks in the City of London and throughout south-east England in the dioceses of Rochester, Canterbury, Chichester and Winchester. William Hokiton was also the Prior who initiated plans around 1345 for the building of a new church. Given local popular support and a vibrant Community, there would have been energy and optimism for such a project, and on 13 September 1348 (the Vigil of the Feast of the Holy Cross), the Bishop of Llandaff blessed the site of the cemetery and the new church. The Bishop, John Pashcal, was a Carmelite and had begun his religious life in the Carmelite priory at Ipswich. The church was not consecrated until 1417; one reason for this delay would have been the Black Death, which adversely

affected the economy and decimated the population. However, the de Grey family continued to be generous benefactors. In 1369, John de Rynger of Aylesford endowed a chantry chapel, and the endowment was immediately ratified by the Archbishop of Canterbury.

However, the Community was not just bricks and mortar. The Prior at this time, Robert St Alban, spent some of the priory's income on the library. He bought manuscripts from the parish priest of Aylesford, John Miller, and also used money from a legacy received from the Rector of Hunton to further build up the stock of books. In 1381 a list of volumes was drawn up: there were 75 volumes including Bibles, writings of St Augustine and the Sentences of Peter Lombard bound in white leather. While Robert St Alban was Prior, the Bishop of Rochester, Thomas Brinton, preached at the Priory in the presence of Baron de Grey on 25 March 1374. The Bishop's sermon was on Our Lady, and the text still exists in a collection of his sermons. Thomas Brinton was originally a Benedictine monk and proved to be a committed pastoral bishop.

One of the more distinguished members of the Order linked to Aylesford Priory is Richard of Maidstone. Richard, a doctor of divinity who had studied at Oxford, was a great controversialist who crossed swords with the Wycliffites. While he was at Oxford he wrote two works attacking the views of John Ashwardby, vicar of St Mary's, the University church in Oxford. Ashwardby had criticised the mendicant orders from his pulpit and urged his congregation to withhold alms from the Friars.

Richard's counter-argument was that friars renounce all property so that they can be free to evangelise the world; mendicancy is a consequence of the renunciation of property. Richard of Maidstone became confessor to John of Gaunt, the powerful Duke of Lancaster, and is recorded as writing a poem to celebrate the reconciliation of Richard II and the people of London. Richard is of interest as a religious poet and his meditative translations of the penitential psalms were wrongly attributed to Richard Rolle. It is interesting that despite his disputes with the Wycliffites, he was happy to be influenced by Wycliffe's translations of the scriptures. The psalms were meant as an aid to the devotional lives of lay people and indicate that the scriptures were being opened up to the laity, as well as to clerics, long before the Reformation. The following prayer from this work gives a flavour of the style, which is not unlike that of Chaucer:

Bot, Lord that boghtest man so dere,
Let him no blys in balys bring,
But sende hym myght to amende hym here,
And graunt to hym grace of uprysyng.

Richard of Maidstone died in 1396 and is buried at The Friars.

A Provincial Chapter was held at Aylesford in 1407. Thomas Netter, an Essex man, was Provincial, and Professor David Knowles described him as perhaps the most distinguished friar of his time. Netter was a confidant of Henry IV and Henry V but he was also a considerable theologian. His writings against Wycliffe were definitive and his other works were influential in the Order down the years. Netter guided the Province for many years and presided over a golden age, a time when the Order flourished and produced some outstanding friars. Shortly after this chapter the Carmelites began to build quite extensively at Aylesford – new cloisters sprang up and many other buildings were radically renovated.

In June 1415, Stephan Patryngton was consecrated Bishop of St David's at All Saints, Maidstone by Henry Chichelle, Archbishop of Canterbury. Stephan was one of many distinguished Carmelite friars of the period. A Yorkshireman, he studied at Oxford and was a prolific writer and apologist. He was to be present at the Council of Constance and in 1417 he was

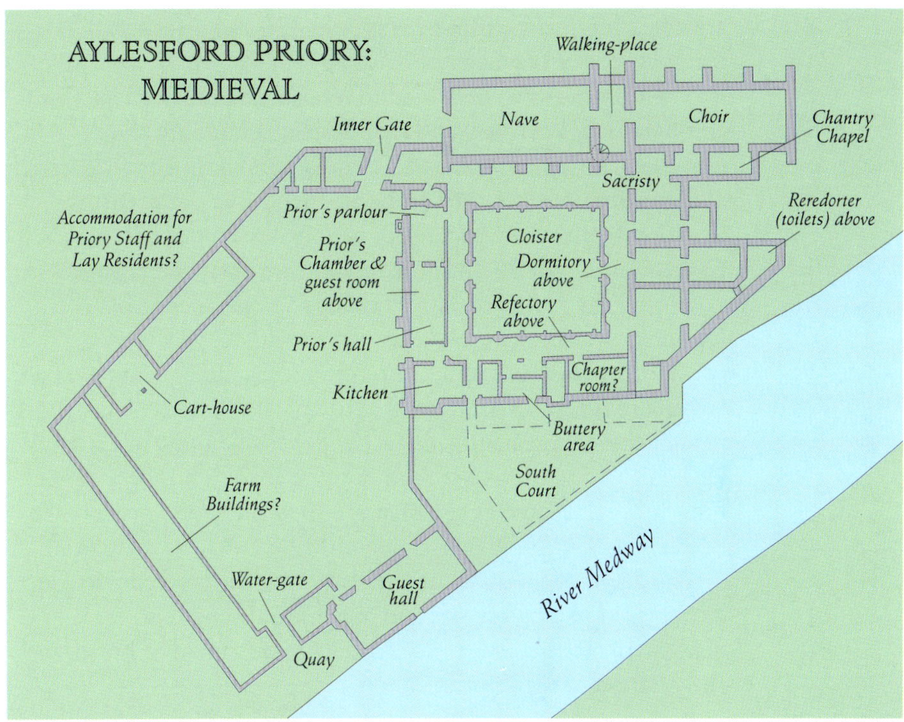

appointed Bishop of Chichester. However, he died shortly after his translation to Chichester.

May 1417 saw the dedication of the new church. Richard Young, the Bishop of Rochester, presided at the dedication and also consecrated various altars in the Church, to St John the Baptist and SS Peter and Paul. He granted 40 days' indulgence to all who supported the Carmelites at Aylesford.

Another Provincial Chapter was held at Aylesford in 1443 when Nicholas Kenton was elected Provincial. In 1445 the same Nicholas Kenton gave John Kemp, the Archbishop of York, permission to stay at The Friars. John Kemp was a Cardinal and also protector of the Carmelite Order. Like many prelates of the period, he was involved in secular politics, being twice Lord Chancellor of England and ending his life as Archbishop of Canterbury. Why did he stay at The Friars? It would be a pious thought to think he needed time to stop and be peaceful. Some few years later in 1458 Thomas Bouchier, Archbishop of Canterbury, stayed at the Priory while visiting parishes in the area. It is interesting that he stayed at The Friars rather than using his palace in Maidstone.

The Community continued to receive generous benefactions throughout the century and this enabled rebuilding and refurbishing work to continue. Benefactors came from the length and breadth of the county, from Sittingbourne in the east to Cowden in the west. Bequests continued to come to the Community right up until the dissolution of the monasteries.

During the Spring of 1469, Thomas Scrope, Bishop of Dromore, was in Kent. He ordained candidates to the ministry at All Saints, Maidstone and Canterbury Cathedral. Thomas was a Carmelite who had annoyed his Provincial, Thomas Netter, with his sensational preaching about the Second Coming of Christ. He lived for a while as a recluse but was made a bishop by Pope Eugene IV and acted as suffragan to the Bishop of Norwich. He lived a long and varied life, dying in 1491.

The dawn of the sixteenth century saw the death of Henry de Grey, the last baron, the end of a line of friends and benefactors to the Order. He willed that he should be buried in the Chancel of the Priory Church.

STORM CLOUDS GATHER

In 1505, Peter Terrasse, the Prior General, visited Aylesford. He was a Catalan by birth and had been elected Prior General at a Chapter held in Piacenza in 1503. Terrasse made every effort to visit the different houses of the Order, but he was no reformer. He did little to raise standards and granted friars academic degrees without any record of studies being pursued. It seems that Terrasse was more interested in collecting funds than trying to improve the quality of religious observance. By the time of his visit, the English Province of Carmelites had lost much of its vigour and the death of Thomas Scrope marked the end of an era which had produced many distinguished Carmelites. The Order still attracted novices, but the quality of those coming forward was not high. John Bale, the great chronicler of the Carmelites in England, who ended his life in 1563 as a Canon of Canterbury Cathedral, wrote in 1536: 'Today there are few men of learning among them and few still who are men of virtue.'

If Terrasse had been a reformer, would the Carmelites at the time of the Reformation have made a more spirited stance against the royal decrees? A sad example of declining standards is shown in an incident that took place in the Nottingham Priory in 1532 when William Bachon and Roger Sherwood, the Prior, quarrelled while drinking – the Prior struck his confrere, who died the following day!

Local people continued to support the friars but by 1534 the clouds were looming. That year all the friars had to make an oath of allegiance to King Henry and Queen Anne, and to swear that the Pope had no more authority than any other Bishop. Besides this their sermons were to be examined for their doctrinal content and burnt if not Catholic, sound and orthodox. In addition to the oath an inventory had to be made of precious objects and moveable goods. In 1535, the commissioners visited The Friars. The Community held 18 acres of land worth 42s 6d a year: this seems to have been a low estimate. The end came on 13 December 1538, when Richard Ingworth received the house of White Friars at Aylesford into the King's hands. Ingworth was himself a former Dominican Friar, now Bishop of Dover. So the English Province of Carmelite Friars came to an end and despite heroic efforts over the years it was 1926 before the Carmelite Friars were firmly re-established in England.

As the friars left Aylesford the future must have looked bleak. Those who were ordained could look for chaplaincies or parishes but any brothers would have been hard put to find a future. Some English Carmelites were among the earliest enthusiasts for the Reformation, especially those who studied in Cambridge in the 1520s. John Barrett from Lynn in Norfolk left the Order along with John Bale in 1533 and functioned as a parish priest in Norfolk. The Provincial, John Bird, wrote a treatise in favour of the King's divorce. Bird became Bishop of Bangor but under Mary he accepted Roman obedience again and acted as suffragan to Bishop Bonner of London. John Bale was the most extreme in support of the new order, using his talents as a playwright to write propaganda for the Protestant cause. We owe a debt to Bale for his attempts to chronicle the history of the Medieval Carmelite Province. Under Edward VI he was Bishop of Ossary (Kilkenny) in Ireland and after exile under Mary he spent his last years as a Canon of Canterbury.

Thomas Cromwell wrote to Sir Thomas Wyatt in February 1539, 'I have reserved for you the house of the Friars of Aylesford.' The Wyatts, of Allington Castle at Maidstone, had been loyal supporters of the Tudors, and Thomas Wyatt was a poet and diplomat of some distinction. He was well rewarded: he received possession of the Cistercian Abbey at Boxley as well as the Benedictine Convent at West Malling. Some ruins of Boxley Abbey can still be glimpsed from the motorway, but West Malling Abbey once again functions as a religious house.

The Wyatts never lived at Aylesford. In fact in 1542 the property was leased to John Morse for 40 years at an annual rent of 102 shillings. Some of the buildings had already been leased before the Dissolution. Thomas Wyatt died in 1542 and was succeeded by his son, Thomas Wyatt the Younger.

The turbulent politics of the period cast a shadow over this part of Kent. Thomas Wyatt opposed the accession of Mary to

Left:
Alms-houses in Aylesford village

the throne and joined the Kent Rebellion in 1554. The Rebellion was crushed by forces loyal to the Queen and the ringleaders executed. The Friars was forfeited to the Crown and was eventually granted in 1570 to John Sedley of Southfleet. John Sedley was to live at the Priory until his death in 1605. He married Anne Colepeper, strengthening his Kentish links by the marriage.

John Sedley began to turn the monastic buildings into a country house. He demolished the church and the section of the cloister near to the river. He then remodelled the rest of the buildings, putting in new windows. The refectory wing over the Cloister Chapel was divided into three floors and the gate-house was built in 1595. The water-gate area was improved, providing accommodation for Sedley's steward, and it is possible that Sedley also built a farmhouse on the site of what is now Lodge Farm. There is a tradition that some of the stone from the church found its way to Upnor and was used for the strengthening of the fortifications at Upnor Castle. Another tradition has it that Sir Walter Raleigh stayed at The Friars towards the end of the sixteenth century.

John Sedley died in 1605 and, as he was childless, his brother Sir William Sedley JP inherited the property. John Sedley's will made provision for the poor of the locality, stating that a house be built for six poor, aged persons and setting aside some £60 per annum for the upkeep of the residents. His brother, William, proved to be a faithful executor, building the alms-houses in Aylesford Village and adding to the endowment so that there was now £76 per annum available for the poor, meaning that seven poor persons could be cared for. The hospital was dedicated to the Holy Trinity. Henry Brassey added to the alms-houses so that 15 people could find accommodation. The buildings have recently been modernised and are a lasting memorial to the Sedleys.

William Sedley was made a baronet in 1611, which indicates that he must have been active in the politics of the day. Besides his charitable works it seems that he developed the agricultural side of The Friars. A date carved into the door lintel of the West Barn suggests that this huge barn, recently restored, was built in 1615.

Sir William Sedley died in 1619, leaving bequests to the University Libraries at Oxford and Cambridge and providing an endowment of £2000 to fund a lectureship in Natural Philosophy at Oxford. His son, Sir John Sedley, inherited the baronetcy and The Friars, but was to sell the Priory and 500 acres in 1633 to Sir Peter Rycaut, who came from a Dutch merchant banking background.

The Rycauts were to own The Friars during a turbulent time in English history: in the 1630s, when they acquired it, the tensions that were to lead to the Civil War were already evident. The Rycauts were firm royalists, like most of the landowners and people of Kent, but as the county was so near to London, the Parliamentary forces tried to keep a vice-like grip on the county. Sir Anthony Weldon, the Parliamentary leader of the county, was able and efficient, but also violent and dictatorial. By 1647 the whole county was ready to rise, and 1648 saw a rebellion crushed by Colonel Fairfax at the Battle of Maidstone in June 1648.

In 1642 the Rycauts had begun to store arms and money at The Friars and were also involved with other Royalists in organising opposition to the Parliamentary Committee. Parliament was aware of these subversives and sent Colonel Sandys to suppress any attempts at a rising in Kent. He made two forays into the county. On August 14 he went to Sevenoaks and put paid to a group of Cavaliers headed by Sir John Sackville at Knole, taking five cartloads of weapons and ransacking the house. Five days later he headed off to Rochester, storming the bridge before breaking up the 'superstitious worship' in the Cathedral. Still breathing fire, Colonel Sandys turned his attention to the Catholics in the area. At Birling Manor he found a crucifix, popish books and a picture of the Blessed Virgin Mary, but no weapons.

Sandys then crossed the Medway and searched The Friars, but could find nothing to warrant suspicion. It was only when he was ready to leave that a maid told him of a cache of arms and valuables hidden in the roof. Sir Peter Rycaut was arrested and taken off to Maidstone. He tried to escape while the troopers were having a drink at an inn, but they caught up with him and he was taken to be held at Upnor Castle. In September he was taken to London and was released when he made a loan of £1000 to Parliament. In 1643 he was forced to forfeit his estate to Parliament and was fined £1500. Colonel Sandys' expedition into Kent was successful, but it left a legacy of bitterness in the county. In 1643 over 2000 Cavaliers assembled at Aylesford – among that number were several of Sir Peter's tenants. However, Parliamentary forces defeated them at nearby Yalding.

Kent was now firmly in the power of Parliament and The Friars became the centre of Parliamentarian control in the county. The Committee of Kent, made up of local gentry, was the body designated to ensure that Parliament's will should be supreme in the county. They met twice weekly at The Friars under the decisive chairmanship of Sir Anthony Weldon. Law and Order was their main priority, in particular making sure that

Right: *The Friars depicted in an early seventeenth-century painting by an unknown artist at Packington Hall*

opponents of Parliament were arrested. Another task was the raising and arming of local militia loyal to the Parliamentary cause. However, Kent remained loyal to the King despite these endeavours, as a rising in 1645 proved.

Sir Peter Rycaut was allowed to return to The Friars in 1647, since by that time the Committee had transferred its meetings to The Star in Maidstone. Sir Peter was heavily in debt, having lost five years' income and paid some heavy fines. He also found that the woodlands he owned at New Hythe had been ruined in his absence.

More trouble loomed in 1648 when there was a major rising of Cavaliers in Kent. The Parliamentary leaders fled to The Friars where stores of weapons were still laid up for their use. Sir Peter remained loyal to the King, so the Parliamentarians had to flee leaving arms and ammunition. The Royalist leader was Sir John Anderson, a son-in-law of Sir Peter. However, Colonel Fairfax, the Parliamentary commander, proved a more able strategist than his Cavalier opponents, and he defeated the rebels at Maidstone.

After this fiasco, life for the Rycauts became more and more problematic. In 1650 the Council of State had The Friars searched; the object of the search was the suspicion that the Rycauts were in correspondence with Charles Stuart and other enemies of the Commonwealth. About this time Sir Peter's business collapsed and he became bankrupt. Sir Peter died in 1653 a broken man and he was buried in St Peter's church, Aylesford.

Right:
A staircase built by John Banks at the time of the Restoration

Lady Rycaut was left with a mountain of debt and was forced to sell The Friars and 512 acres of land to John Banks of Maidstone. The selling price was £8413. Paul Rycaut tried to help his mother and brother, but to no avail as John Banks drove a hard bargain with the impoverished family. Paul Rycaut went on to make his name as a writer and traveller, becoming a specialist in Turkish history.

JOHN BANKS: 'KEEP YOUR ACCOUNTS PUNCTUAL'

John Banks, the new owner of The Friars, was a Maidstone man. His grandfather, also named John, was a successful woollen draper who married into a Kentish family of lesser gentry. His father, Caleb, was a leading member of the Maidstone business community. Caleb was a JP, three times Mayor of Maidstone, and had served on the County Committee. He was shrewd and enterprising, always on the lookout for a good deal. John Banks inherited this business acumen and was politic enough to know when he needed to be flexible. In 1654 he married Elizabeth Dethick, the daughter of a City of London merchant and sometime Lord Mayor of London.

***Above:** Portrait of John Banks, attributed to Lely, at Packington Hall*

John Banks laid the foundations of his fortune by becoming part of a syndicate set up to provide food supplies to the Navy. The period 1650–80 saw a series of wars against the Dutch and French that were mainly waged at sea. As a result, the English Navy grew to be the largest industry in the land. Financial checks were not in place so contractors like John Banks had rich pickings. Through his Kent connections he supplied hops, cereal and beef to the Navy as well as importing canvas and saltpetre from France. At the same time he began to underwrite debts, claiming on an average some ten per cent for the risk. In this way he could add about £3000 per year to his income; in modern terms the amount would be reckoned in millions. His marriage into the Dethick family opened trading opportunities to Spain and the New World, and he also began to make cautious investments in the East India Company.

The Restoration of Charles II could have been a difficult time for Banks. He represented Maidstone in the Parliaments of 1654, 1656 and 1659. However, he was pragmatic in his politics and beliefs and was able to swim with the tide. Like many other businessmen, he saw that a restored monarchy would bring stability, which was good for business. An example of his pragmatism (and his access to hard cash) is shown in his willingness to underwrite a debt Charles II had incurred in Holland. For his careful service he was made a baronet in 1661.

Banks divided his time between London and Aylesford, but it was not until he had established his fortune that he carried out major alterations at The Friars. In the 1660s he began to purchase land in Burham, Detling and Boxley and planted fruit trees there. He sold timber and reeds to the Navy and also supplied provisions for an expedition to the Mediterranean. With the profits from these sales he was able to finance the construction of a new barn at Aylesford. While he was in London his father Caleb kept an eye on the Aylesford estate until he died in 1669, leaving his son some £28,000 richer. He had been a shrewd and successful merchant in his lifetime, but was dismissed by the local gentry as a shopkeeper.

Right: *Detail of the ceiling in the Ballroom. Photograph ©* Country Life

James Sherbourne took over the stewardship of the estate in 1672, and about this time Lodge Farm House was built on the site of the old farm building. During the 1660s Banks began the work of transforming the medieval priory into an elegant country house. Samuel Pepys was much impressed by the state of The Friars when he called to see Sir John on 24 March 1669. He was actually in London at the time, but Pepys reported, 'here I had sight of his seat and house the outside which is an old abbey just like Hitchenbrooke, and as good at least, and mighty finely placed by the river; and he keeps the grounds about it and

Left: *The Ballroom. Photograph* © Country Life

the walls and house, very handsome. I was mightily pleased with the sight of it.'

The 1670s were to see Sir John Banks fully established. He became a Governor and Director of the East India Company and bought a large town house in Lincoln's Inn Fields. He was elected MP for Rochester and saw his daughter Elizabeth marry Heneage Finch, who was already an influential Tory politician.

Between 1677 and 1679, as a sign that he was one of the 'great in the land', Banks carried out a massive programme of rebuilding at The Friars. By 1685 he was able to claim that he had spent the best part of £16,000 on 'land, mansion house and park at Aylesford'. Lead rain-water heads against the old refectory and Prior's Hall are dated 1677/78 and coincide with the building expenditures that Sir John recorded in his account books. The Cloisters were enclosed, new windows were put in and the old stone paving was replaced by black and white marble. A new main entrance was made in the East Wing, while the old hall was divided into rooms. The West Wing on the site of the old gatehouse was enlarged to include the fine dining-room. The old refectory became a magnificent ballroom. Here, as elsewhere, beautiful moulded ceilings were put in place, and oak panelling abounded. The decorations of the new ballroom were Dutch in character, which was unusual in England. Mention is made of Inigo Jones being involved, though that could be verified by a careful examination of Sir John's accounts. He was meticulous in recording every expenditure – one of his slogans was 'keep your accounts punctual'. Sir John also paid great attention to the gardens. Signs of this care are shown in the walled garden and Orangery that remain to this day. A final flourish was the stocking of the deer park.

Sir John lived on until 1699, his wife and son Caleb both predeceasing him. Caleb proved a great disappointment: despite the care lavished on his education he was a sickly and indecisive person. John Locke, the philosopher, was his tutor but neither this eminent teacher nor foreign travel did much to help. Elizabeth's husband Heneage Finch was as shrewd as his father-in-law and both survived the upheavals of James II's reign and the Revolution. At his death Sir John Banks had assets of some £200,000 – to some he was still a draper's son but to many others

Opposite: *John Banks' tomb in Aylesford parish church*

Memoriæ Sacrum
Hinc fœlicem expectant Resurrectionem
IOHANNES BANKS de AYLSFORD in Comitatu Cantij Baronett
Uxor etiam ejus ELIZABETHA IOHANNIS Dethick Militis
è Comitatu Norfolciæ, olim Prætoris LONDINENSIS Filia
Necnon Filius utriusq; communis CALEB BANKS
Maritus quidem, sed Liberis orbatus
His præterea nati sunt Liberi quatuor
MARTHA, ELIZABETHA, MARIA, & IOHANNES
Filias tantum duas superstites reliquerunt
ELIZABETHAM & MARIAM MARTHA & IOHANNE extinctis
Quarum altera, nempe ELIZABETHA, nupta fuit
HENEAGIO FINCH, HENEAGIJ COMITIS NOTTINGHAMIÆ
Summi ANGLIÆ CANCELLARIJ Filio natu secundo
auspiciis Serenissimæ REGINÆ ANNÆ BARONI de GERNSEY
MARIA vero IOHANNI SAVILL IOHANNIS de METHLEY
in Comitatu EBORACENSI Armigeri, Filio Primogenito
Exuvias deposuerunt
CALEB BANKS Sepbris 13° An° 1696 Ætat 57
ELIZABETHA Octbris 21° An° 1696 Ætat 59
IOHANNES Octbris 18° An° 1699 Ætat 72

***Above:** The new east entrance as devised by John Banks, illustrated in a colour engraving by G. Shepherd, 1829*

he was living proof that a careful businessman could achieve respectability. He died a temperate Anglican believing God was 'a god of order among men'. He had had little interest in power for its own sake, valuing his membership of the Royal Society and his links with men like Locke and Pepys. Paradoxically he left little in the way of a dynasty. His portrait by Lely shows a certain grandeur, while the elaborate tomb by Nost in St Peter's at Aylesford speaks of wealth. For Maidstone people his memory is preserved by a row of handsome alms-houses in the town centre. As a Carmelite I believe that we owe Sir John a debt of gratitude. His care of The Friars and the extensive rebuilding ensured that it would not become a bare ruined choir. In 1687 the Prior General of Carmelites wrote to King James II and petitioned him to return The Friars to the Order; one wonders whether Sir John Banks was ever aware of that correspondence!

Just over a year after Sir John's death, Sir Paul Rycaut, son of Sir Peter Rycaut, was buried at Aylesford parish church. He has an enduring reputation as a scholar and explorer. He never enjoyed life at The Friars, but Aylesford was his final resting-place.

The Finch family were to be the owners of The Friars for the next two centuries. Heneage Finch was a capable politician holding high office of state. He was created Earl of Aylesford by George I in 1714 and besides being a Privy Councillor he was also Chancellor of the Duchy of Lancaster. The Earl died in 1719, in his 70th year, but his wife Elizabeth lived on until 1743. His son, also called Heneage, was also involved in political life and married into a Warwickshire family, the Fishers. His wife Mary inherited the Fisher estates, including Packington Hall, and some time before the middle of the century the Finches made Packington Hall the family seat, with The Friars becoming the dower-house of the family. The Finch family continued to care for the house and the estate, and sketches made by Thorpe for his study *Antiquities in Kent*, published in 1778, show the gate-house and main courtyard in excellent order. Thorpe also made a plan of The Friars. His notes make interesting reading, as the present day Pilgrims' Hall is listed as a brew-house. At the end of the eighteenth century both Samuel Ireland and Hasted, the Kent historian, make mention of Charlotte, Dowager Countess of Aylesford, living at The Friars. She was the daughter of the Duke of Somerset and died at The Friars in 1805. Her son, the fourth Earl, had a military career and was involved in suppressing the 1798 rebellion in Ireland.

Below: *The gate-house – line drawing by Thorpe, 1778*

The nineteenth century saw a number of tenants living at The Friars, some of whom were retired military officers. For a short period (1874-87) it was again a dower house as the sixth Countess, Jane Knightly, took up residence there. Sir Arthur Evans stayed at The Friars while engaged in excavations of Iron Age and Paleolithic remains in the area. Between 1890 and the turn of the century a number of military men rented the property. Colonel Claude Lowther thought of restoring it but decided to move to Herstmonceux Castle instead. An advertisement in the *Times* of 19 June 1907 announced that The Friars would be sold by auction on 15 July by Harrods:

RESIDENTIAL ESTATE OF 446 ACRES KENT, near Maidstone – An important FREEHOLD RESIDENTIAL PROPERTY, known as The Friars, Aylesford, originally an old Carmelite Priory. It is approached by carriage drive, with a fine old tower gateway, forming lodge. The accommodation comprises entrance hall, music room (44ft by 25ft), four reception rooms, 16 bed and dressing rooms, three bath rooms &c; stabling for nine horses, coachman's and groom's rooms, cottage, beautiful grounds, capital farm of about 200 acres, farmhouse and buildings. Also two other Residences, with grounds, known as The Cedars and Wickham Lodge. Also a fine sand pit and 34 acres of woodland, extending in all to about 446 acres. The whole property, with the exception of the residence and about 35 acres and the woodland, is let, and produces a rental of £1,200 per annum.

Will be SOLD by AUCTION, on July 15th, by HARRODS Ltd, Brompton Road, London. SW.

Clearly the sale never took place, but The Friars suffered a period of neglect in the early years of this century.

***Above:** An engraving of the courtyard, from a line-drawing by Thorpe, 1778*

***Below:** A painting of The Friars from the Walled Garden, dating from 1873*

A NEW DAWN

During the First World War, Mrs Woolsey rented The Friars from the Earl of Aylesford's Estate, and she continued to live there until her death in 1931. She had a great love of old buildings and began to lavish her time, care and money on

Left: *Mrs Copley Hewitt*

***Above:** Mr Copley Hewitt (right) and Lord Baden-Powell (centre)*

The Friars. Her daughter Alice and her husband Mr Copley Hewitt came to live at The Friars in 1920 and the house came to life again. Lord Martin Conway, writing in *Country Life* in 1923, observed that 'since the present tenant has been in occupation much has been done to bring the building into much-needed repair and to embellish the charmingly laid out old gardens without any interference with the mellowed work of successive generations who have made this charming and charmingly situated house their home. Few houses in England offer examples and such good examples of the work of so many generations or so picturesque and harmonious a group of styles.' Lord Conway's only caveat was the presence of ivy on the buildings. Certainly the photographs that accompany the articles show the house in good order.

Mr Copley Hewitt was a person of some importance in the life of Kent. He worked in the City of London as a Commissioner for the Inland Revenue. However, in 1929–30 he was High

Sheriff for Kent and also Assistant County Commissioner for the Scouts. He served as a governor of Dover College. His wife Alice was involved with Guides and Brownies, so it is little wonder that The Friars became an important centre for scouting activities. The Pilgrims' Hall became the venue for scouting meetings. Lord Baden-Powell visited The Friars in 1926 and gave Mr Copley Hewitt the Badge of Silver Wolf, the highest honour in scouting.

Father Malachy Lynch, in his newsletter of September 1965, records an interesting incident. The Carmelites returned to Kent in 1926, taking over the Roman Catholic parishes of Faversham and Sittingbourne. The Prior General of the Order, Father Elias Maginnis, came to visit Kent and came over to The Friars in the company of Father Elias Lynch. There was a Girl Guide jamboree taking place at the time, with the Archbishop of Canterbury present as a distinguished guest. Father Malachy describes the visit with great warmth: 'Mrs Copley Hewitt gave a great

Below: *The aftermath of the fire at The Friars*

welcome to the Prior General. Despite all the other distinguished visitors on that occasion she clung on to him eagerly and they got on very well together. This was not surprising. He was a personality… I remember Mrs Hewitt as a spiritual woman – gentle and wistful and aware of the timelessness of prayer.'

29 June 1930 was a black day in the history of The Friars – fire broke out during the night. Fortunately, one of the staff woke up to give the alarm and ensured that everyone escaped unharmed. Fire engines came from Maidstone and Chatham but a large portion of the house was destroyed. The beautiful moulded ceilings were lost, along with the lovely main staircase. Mrs Woolsey, now an old lady, sat disconsolately near the gate-house watching the house she loved burning. Volunteers carried out valuable paintings and furniture but many treasures were lost. The south and west wings of the Cloisters were gutted, and a contemporary photograph shows the stone skeleton that remained. Fortunately, the north wing and the courtyard survived, but the devastation was overwhelming. Mrs Woolsey never recovered from the shock and died six months later in January 1931. After the initial shock was past, Mr and Mrs Copley Hewitt began the work of restoration. Mr Copley Hewitt negotiated the purchase of The Friars from the estate of the Earls of Aylesford. The trustees of the estate moved quite slowly but by March 1932 the purchase was completed, and the restoration work subsequently carried out by the Copley Hewitts restored The Friars to its medieval monastic style. The cloisters were restored to their fifteenth-

ST. MARY'S COLLEGE BUILDING & MISSIONARY FUND

Custodian Trustee:
BARCLAY'S BANK LTD.

Managing Trustees:
V. Rev. J. C. Fitzgerald, O.C. Prov.
V. Rev. M. E. Lynch, O.C.
V. Rev. W. M. Lynch, O.C.
V. Rev. P. L. Geary, O.C.
V. Rev. C. B. Fitzgerald, O.C.
V. Rev. P. E. Scally, O.C.

WHITEFRIARS
FAVERSHAM
KENT

20 June 1949

This morning at 12/30 pm, was signed in the presence of the following people, the contract for purchase of the Friars Aylesford on behalf of the Calced Carmelites.

M. Elias Lynch. O.Carm Faversham
D. A. [illegible] solicitor Sittingbourne
P. Edwin Scally; O. Carm, Prior, Faversham
B. L. Cogan O.Carm. prior, Sittingbourne
[illegible] Hastings O.Carm. Sittingbourne
P Leo Maher O.Carm Lay Brother Sittingbourne
P. Anthony McGreal O.Carm. Lay Brother Faversham
Carmelite Priory
Sittingbourne Kent.

Above: *The document ratifying the sale of The Friars*

century splendour and the old refectory at their west end was given a splendid Gothic window. Timbers from the old training ship *Arethusa* were used for the new roof over the old refectory. The *Arethusa* was first launched in 1845 and had recently been broken up in 1934.

Mr Copley Hewitt was not able to complete all the work of restoring The Friars. The outbreak of war made things difficult and in September 1941 Mr Copley Hewitt died at the age of 70. The war years saw servicemen billeted at The Friars but there was no bomb damage, despite Kent being in the frontline during the Battle of Britain. One highlight of the war years was the dances held in the restored refectory. There are still people alive who have nostalgic memories of those days.

Mrs Alice Copley Hewitt died in 1947. While her husband was busy repairing fire damage, she was able to bring the old chapel in the south wing into use again for worship. In 1935 the Bishop of Rochester gave permission for acts of worship to take place in the chapel, and a plaque in what is now the Cloister Chapel records this permission.

After Mrs Copley Hewitt's death, Major Woolsey Hewitt put the property on the market. Ever since the Carmelites returned to Kent in 1926, they had hoped that one day The Friars would belong again to the Order. Negotiations for the purchase were conducted on 20 June 1949, the cost being agreed at £25,000. The money for the purchase came through an appeal initiated by Father Kilian Lynch, the Prior General. The documentation includes the signature of Father Elias Lynch who had visited The Friars back in 1929 with the then Prior General. Another signatory was Mr Ardizzone, the Order's solicitor, a cousin of the famous illustrator Edward Ardizzone. Among the other signatories was Brother Anthony McGreal, a Carmelite who had been involved in raising the money for the purchase of The Friars. Various parts of the property had tenants: Mrs Wellman had a portion of the courtyard as 'a cottage', as did Lt Roberts RN. The Copley Hewitts were most helpful in enabling the Carmelites to return to their old home and the Order owes the family a debt of gratitude.

CHEQUERS INN.
KENTS BEST ALES
WINES & SPIRITS

The Carmelite friars returned to The Friars on 31 October 1949. The procession of some 50 friars wended its way over the old stone bridge, through the village and down through the gate-house. The restored refectory with its new Gothic window and the great beams from the *Arethusa* now made a fine chapel. After a vigil of prayer, Mass was celebrated on All Saints' Day, 1 November, and Father Malachy Lynch was installed as Prior by his brother Father Kilian Lynch, the Prior General of the Order.

Father Malachy Lynch is a key figure in the restoration of Aylesford. He came from County Wicklow in Ireland and was one of three brothers who all became Carmelite friars. He was among the first Carmelites to arrive in Kent in 1926 and came to love the county. From 1936 until 1949 he worked in Wales doing education and missionary work. He was a person of deep spirituality, with a great gift for recognising artistic talent. He was an avid reader and a keen listener – in short, a person of vision and culture.

Left: *The courtyard in 1949*

Opposite: *The Carmelites process through Aylesford village*

Father Malachy was to prove an ideal choice as Prior, and for the next decade and beyond his influence shaped the work of restoration. The original idea was that The Friars should become a centre of studies for the Carmelite Order; however, events were to lead the Priory's development down a different road. Photographs taken in 1949 show the restoration work carried out by Mr Copley Hewitt but they also evidence the effects of the War and its aftermath. Many of the buildings in the courtyard needed repair as maintenance was well nigh impossible during the War and in subsequent years. Father Malachy had only a small community of friars and a band of lay helpers that included the newly formed Institute of Our Lady of Mount Carmel. The 'Sisters', as they were called, lived in the gatehouse, and the Friars found space in the main building. Over the next few years the buildings were transformed. A kitchen area was built and the Pilgrims' Hall was once again a centre for hospitality for visitors. In the period from 1538–1949 it has been a barn, a brew-house, an armoury and a scout HQ. Money and building materials were in short supply, but with Father Malachy's great gift for begging, and a sense of trust, the work went ahead. In 1951 the remains of St Simon Stock were brought back from Bordeaux to find a

***Below:** The temporary altar*

final resting-place in Kent. The ceremony took place on 16 July with many notable people in attendance. The Archbishop of Bordeaux handed the relics to the Bishop of Southwark, Mgr Cyril Cowderoy, on the old stone bridge. Then a great procession set off to The Friars with the whole village *en fête*. The vicar made the primary school available for the clergy to vest – a most generous gesture. Among the dignitaries present was Éamon De Valera, the Irish statesman. The crowds that flocked to The Friars for the occasion were to become the norm, because The Friars, not by design but by popular choice, was fast becoming a centre for pilgrimage. The first group of pilgrims came from Ealing Abbey in 1950 and soon large groups were coming every Sunday.

The community of friars began to grow, and soon workshops and a farm were established. Father Malachy, influenced by the Ditchling Community, believed that art and beauty were essential for religion. Soon there was a whole group of craftsmen – lay and secular – working at The Friars. Brother Aloysius, a German Carmelite, made tables for the Pilgrims' Hall. He was soon joined by Charlie Bodiam who was to work at The Friars for many years as a carpenter. Father Brocard Sewell set up a printing press, producing elegant books in the tradition of Ditchling. A pottery was established, directed for many years by Brother Michael McMullen. The pots had a simple beauty and wonderful glazes, the secrets of which had been bequeathed by the famous potter, Bernard Leech. A farm and market garden began to flourish thanks to the hard work of two Spanish Carmelites, Nunio and Simon.

Besides their involvement in crafts at The Friars, artists were also enlisted to add dignity to the restoration work. Philip Lindsay Clarke and his son Michael used their talents as sculptors in their own right, but Philip Lindsay Clarke's greatest contribution was to introduce Adam Kossowski to Father Malachy Lynch. Adam had had a distinguished artistic and academic career in Poland but had suffered badly during the War, being imprisoned in Central Asia by the Soviets. His first commission was for seven tempera paintings depicting the history of the Carmelites, and these now hang in the Chapter Room. Father Malachy then asked Adam to make 15 ceramics

***Right:** The construction of the new shrine and chapels*

depicting the Mysteries of the Rosary, to make a garden of prayer for pilgrims. Kossowski carried out the commission with some apprehension as it was his first experience of working in that medium on such a scale, but the work was a success and he worked on at Aylesford, mainly in ceramics, for some 20 years. Father Malachy saw the work as a twentieth-century expression of the spirit of Della Robbia.

Funding these projects was never easy, but the money always came in the end. In 1951 Father Malachy bought Allington Castle, two miles upstream from The Friars, the former home of Sir Thomas Wyatt. The castle became a flourishing retreat centre and remained in Carmelite hands until 1996.

The number of pilgrims gave rise to the question of rebuilding the medieval church. The old foundations had been uncovered but the decision of whether or not to rebuild was not an easy one to take. Finally, in 1958, a design by Adrian Gilbert Scott was adopted. He designed a large outdoor shrine area with chapels radiating off this central shrine. Work began in 1958 with a few craftsmen and a band of volunteers helped by the young friars. Percy Kitchen, the foreman, was a key figure, loyal and resourceful. Mention must also be made of the Italian stonemasons who were crucial to the enterprise. Despite difficulties with the foundations because the building was so near to the river, work progressed well. Father Malachy wrote enthusiastically saying it was 'jumping up'. In July 1959 work was well enough advanced for an ordination service to be held in the partly built shrine. The Bishop of Southwark at the time, Mgr Cowderoy, was a great supporter of the Friars and was never happier than when he could be with the Community.

Father Malachy's health began to suffer from the mammoth task, and in 1959 his brother, Father Kilian, who had been Prior General, took over as Prior. He continued the work, helped by Father Malachy, and in July 1965 Cardinal Heenan came to preside at a solemn pontifical Mass of rededication and consecration of the shrine. Later that year the River Medway flooded The Friars, causing immense damage to the Courtyard area; as a flood it was far more serious that the one that had occurred in 1953. Father Richard Hearne, the new Prior, was able

Left: *Father Malachy Lynch*

to oversee the repair work and began a programme of refurbishing the part of the house occupied by the Community. A fine library was established in the old refectory area over the cloister and conference facilities were established in the new block. The fine conventual library owes much to the patient work of Father Brocard Sewell. Father Brocard had worked for G.K. Chesterton and had also been associated with Hillaire Belloc. Through the *Aylesford Review*, which he edited in the 1950s and 60s, Father Brocard brought many literary figures to The Friars. Among his friends and colleagues were Henry Williamson, Colin Wilson, Muriel Spark and Gabriel Fielding. He also was a kind friend to young artists such as Frances Horovitz, Jane Percival and Andrew Sinclair.

Father Malachy Lynch died in May 1972, worn out by the work of re-establishing The Friars as a Carmelite priory. At his funeral, Father Edward Maguire, who was to be Prior in the 1980s, asked the question 'What manner of man was Father Malachy? I would like to think a combination of medieval mystic and a Renaissance Prince – he was never daunted.'

In the years since his death, the Carmelite Friars who make up the Community at Aylesford have tried to build on Father Malachy's vision. Some, like Brother John Berridge who joined the Community almost at its re-founding, are a living memory of the excitement of the early days of restoration.

THE FRIARS TODAY

In the last two decades the work of rebuilding has continued but another vital thing has happened. The Friars has become more and more part of the life – both religious and social – of the county of Kent. The growing work for Christian Unity has seen The Friars become a centre for dialogue and exchange. Relations with the Church of England, especially the Diocese of Rochester, have become warm, with Bishops David Say, Michael Turnball and Michael Nazir Ali being frequent visitors. Anglicans, Methodists, Baptists and members of the URC all come on retreat, while interfaith dialogue with Jews and Muslims is part of the whole enterprise. An ecumenical highlight was Wellsprings in June 1995 when all the churches in Kent had a day to celebrate the richness of our Christian traditions. Among those present were Dr George Carey, Archbishop of Canterbury, and Dr Richard Holloway, Bishop of Edinburgh.

Below: *The seventeenth-century tithe barn, now a tea-room and shop*

The present Archbishop of Southwark, Michael Bowen, has continued to give the same generous support shown by his predecessor. The Carmelites were delighted when in July 1995, Archbishop Bowen chose to celebrate his Silver Jubilee of Episcopal Ordination at The Friars. Cardinal Hume preached at the Mass in the presence of the Papal Nuncio, Cardinal Winning, Archbishop Brady of Armagh and many English Bishops along with a vast crowd of priests and people.

Besides religious services, countless organisations enjoy using the facilities at The Friars for meetings and celebrations. The ambulance service, the St John Ambulance Brigade, the fire brigade and many other groups find a home at The Friars. The beauty of the place and the wonderful works of art have also attracted the media, and over the last few years BBC and ITV have broadcast a number of wonderfully made programmes from The Friars. In 1997, as the 1400th

Above: *A view of the piazza, showing the medieval foundations* ***Below:*** *The relic chapel*